GOD'S BOOK ABOUT DEMONS

— Roger Ellsworth —

GOD'S BOOK ABOUT DEMONS

A ROGER ELLSWORTH CLASSICS COLLECTION BOOK

God's Book about Demons
Roger Ellsworth

ISBN: 978-1-964335-02-5

In this series

God's Book about Angels
God's Book about Heaven
God's Book about Demons

Published by www.greatwriting.org

www.rogerellsworth.org

Dedication

My Pastor,

Dr. Scott Gilbert,

A true man of the Word

With Thanks

Writing has always been for me a team effort. I'm very grateful for my wife, Sylvia, who has been on my team in every way for many years. And, as always, I'm grateful for the wise counsel and kind assistance of my longtime friend, Jim Holmes.

Introduction

For one to say he or she believes in demons is to invite scorn and ridicule. How can anyone with a smidgen of intelligence believe in something so antiquated and medieval? Yes, people used to believe in demons, but they were benighted, unenlightened folks who had to grope around for some explanation of inexplicable evil that came their way. Those times, now long centuries ago, were pre-scientific and pre-enlightenment.

But the smug dismissal of former generations and their beliefs is not without problems. For one thing, there is still evil—plenty of it! No one can deny that. So, what is our explanation for it? Is it just some hitch or glitch in the ol' evolutionary process? To put it another way, how can scientific, intellectual men and women explain the fact that in our "enlightened" times, people constantly and abundantly wage war, murder, rape, steal, and lie?

Perhaps the matter is not as open-and-shut as the proud intellectuals would have us believe. The more intently we gaze at our disjointed world, the more it seems that the teachings of the Bible about evil are right on target. And what does the Bible teach about it? Among other things, it says evil is fostered, engineered, and encouraged by evil masterminds who take great delight in stirring it up and watching it wreak its havoc.

Who are these evil masterminds? The Bible calls them demons. And how are we to define them? Wayne Grudem gives us this simple and clear answer:

Demons are evil angels who sinned against God and who now continually work evil in the world.[1]

If these beings—the demons—are real, it would seem to be wise to acquaint ourselves with what they are like so we can be on guard against them and their devices.

---

1 Wayne Grudem, *Systematic Theology*, Inter-Varsity Press (Leicester, UK), 1994, .412.

Part I—The Master Demon

1

From Lucifer to Satan

Please Read:
Isaiah 14:12–14

How is it that we have demons in this world? The Bible pulls back the curtain that shrouds eternity past to give us a peek into heaven itself. God the Father is there. God the Son is there. God the Holy Spirit is there. And angels are there, lots of angels.

When we think of angels, we must always remember that they are created beings. God is the only uncreated being. The Bible affirms God's creation of the angels with these words:

> Praise Him, all His angels; . . .
> Let them praise the name of the LORD,
> For He commanded and they were created.
> (Ps. 148:2,5)

God created a great number of angels. Hebrews 12:22 says they are "innumerable." Revelation 5:11 says there are "ten thousand times ten thousand and thousands of thousands."

God also created different kinds of angels. The Bible identifies cherubim, seraphim, thrones, dominions, principalities, and powers. In addition to these, it mentions an archangel. How great God is in wisdom and strength to be able to create such beings!

Why did God make the angels? The Bible says they were

made to do His pleasure (Psalm 103:21) and to minister to the saints of God (Hebrews 1:14).

The Glorious Lucifer

Of all the angels God created, one was quite obviously above all the rest. His name was Lucifer, which means "morning star" or "day star." We see something of his greatness and his standing in what the Lord God said to him:

> You were the seal of perfection,
> Full of wisdom and perfect in beauty . . .
> You were the anointed cherub who covers; . . .
> You were perfect in your ways
> from the day you were created, . . .
> (Ezek. 28:12,14,15)

What a glorious being! Lucifer was filled with wisdom. He was perfect in beauty. He enjoyed a special status—"the anointed cherub who covers." Jonathan Edwards writes:

> . . . by the covering cherub is meant the cherub next to the throne of God himself, having a place in the very holy of holies.[2]

Edwards adds:

> . . . this cherub . . . is spoken of as being alone entitled to this great honour and nearness to God's throne in heaven, that he was anointed to be above his fellows.[3]

2 Jonathan Edwards, *The Works of Jonathan Edwards* (Edinburgh, UK: The Banner of Truth Trust, 1988), vol. ii, 609.
3 Edwards, vol. ii, 609.

The Proud Lucifer
•••••••••••••••••••••••

But Lucifer did not keep his exalted position. Why did he not keep it? Isaiah's prophecy gives the answer in the form of a fivefold "I." Lucifer said in his heart:

I will ascend into heaven,
I will exalt my throne above the stars of God;
I will also sit on the mount of the congregation.
I will ascend above the heights of the clouds,
I will be like the Most High.
(Isa. 14:13–14)

Sin originated with Lucifer, and in his sin we see the very essence of sin, namely, it has an "I" right in the middle of it. Filled with himself, his power, his wisdom, and his beauty, Lucifer was no longer content to serve the Lord. He would overthrow God and take His place!

Some have offered a more detailed suggestion about the nature of Lucifer's sin. They understand it in terms of God announcing to the angels that He, God, was going to create mankind, that mankind would fall into sin, and that the Second Person of the Trinity would take humanity to Himself in order to redeem mankind. God further announced that all the angels of heaven would be required to worship and serve Christ in His humanity and also be required to serve as ministering spirits to men. And Lucifer could not bear this. He regarded it as being beneath him and rebelled.

Jonathan Edwards writes of Lucifer:

But when it was revealed to him, high and glorious as he was, that he must be a ministering spirit to the race of mankind which he had seen newly created, which appeared so feeble, mean, and despicable, so vastly inferior, not only to him, the prince of the angels, and head of the created universe, but also to the inferior angels, and he must be subject to one of that race that should hereafter be born, he could not bear it. This occasioned his fall. . .[4]

While we cannot pronounce on the precise set of circumstances at the time of Lucifer's sin, we do know that the very essence of it was pride (1 Tim. 3:6). Is it any wonder that this sin is so very hateful to God? It was the first sin, and it is the root of all sin.

The Fallen Lucifer

We also know that Lucifer was joined in his sin by one-third of the original angels (Rev. 12:4). Needless to say, this ill-conceived rebellion didn't succeed. It resulted in Lucifer and the rebellious angels being cast out of heaven (Isa. 14:12). The book of Revelation describes this rebellion in this way:

And war broke out in heaven: Michael and his angels fought with the dragon: and the dragon and his angels fought, but they did not prevail, nor was a place found for them in heaven any longer. So the great dragon was cast out, that serpent of old, called the Devil and Satan, who deceives the whole world; he was cast to the earth, and his angels were cast out with him.
(Rev. 12:7–9)

We should note that the Michael (meaning "Who is

4 Edwards, vol. ii, 610.

like unto God?") in those verses is none other than God's archangel. He is one of only three angels whose names are given in Scripture. The other two? One is Gabriel ("God's hero" or "Mighty one"), and, of course, Lucifer. But Lucifer lost his name. The conflict in heaven resulted in him no longer being Lucifer. It caused him to get a new name—Satan, which means "Adversary." The other name that the Bible commonly gives him is "the devil," which means "Slanderer."

His defeat in heaven also resulted in him launching a new career. He abandoned his career of being near to God and serving Him, and took up the career of opposing Him on earth.

But there is more to the fall of Lucifer than Lucifer himself. We must not forget the angels who joined him in his rebellion against God. They were cast out of heaven along with him, and they are now known not as angels, but as demons. And they, taking their orders from Satan, are at work on this earth to advance his agenda. They make up his evil empire, as we shall see a bit later.

The rebellion and fall of Lucifer raises thorny questions. Why did God not prevent Lucifer from rebelling? After choosing to allow him to rebel, why did God not immediately confine him in the Lake of Fire? In other words, why did God allow the fallen Lucifer to enter upon his career as Satan the adversary who opposes and resists the work and the rule of God?

In this life, we will never be able to satisfactorily answer all the questions that come to mind about God and His ways. We must be content to see part of the truth and to believe that all of the truth will finally be revealed. Furthermore, we must believe that when that truth is revealed, it will make perfect sense.

2

Satan in Eden

Please Read:
Genesis 3:1–6

After his fall from heaven, Satan showed up in the Garden of Eden. The prophet Ezekiel says to Satan: "You were in Eden, the garden of God" (Ezek. 28:13).

Ezekiel states it, but Genesis 3 gives the details. This is one of the most fascinating chapters in the Bible. It's impossible to understand the world's history or the world's present condition apart from this very old chapter of the Bible. Our world is as it is because Satan went to the Garden of Eden. Without Genesis 3, we are hopelessly jumbled in trying to understand this world.

Why did Satan go there? Adam and Eve were there. They were made by God and for God. They were made in God's image, and they were designed to live for His glory.

Since Satan couldn't defeat God in heaven, his only other option was to defeat Him on earth. To do this, he, Satan, had to focus his attack on Adam and Eve. His desire was to get them to rebel against the God who had made them and blessed them in so many ways. The creatures rebelling against their Creator—Satan would see this as a terrible defeat for God!

So let's go to the Garden of Eden for a visit. The first thing we see is this:

How Satan Appeared

The account of Satan in Eden begins with these words:

> Now the serpent was more cunning than any beast
> of the field which the LORD God had made.
> (Gen. 3:1)

Don't let this serpent throw you. This was none other than Satan himself using the serpent for his evil purpose. The serpent in Eden was Satan taking over the body of the creature known as the serpent. It was very fitting that Satan would choose this particular creature. The creature was the most cunning or crafty of all the animals, and Satan relies on craftiness to advance his cause. Because Satan so successfully used the serpent in Eden, the Bible sometimes simply identifies him as "the serpent" (2 Cor. 11:3) or "that serpent of old" (Rev. 12:9, 20:2).

Satan knew he couldn't come charging into Eden to announce to Adam and Eve that he was there to get them to rebel against God and, in so doing, bring misery upon themselves and their descendants. He knew that wouldn't work. He also knew that what couldn't be done by openly calling Adam and Eve to rebel could be achieved by trickery.

How Satan Approached

The stage is set. Satan moves in. He approaches Eve. Why Eve? By focusing on her, Satan was already attacking God before he ever said a single word. God had ordained that Adam was to lead. Many don't like this teaching of male headship. But if we believe, as we should, that this is God's world, we must surely go on to say that He can govern it just as He pleases.

So God had established a certain order in the first home, and Satan targeting Eve was a direct challenge to that order.

Satan's purpose, of course, was to get Adam and Eve to disobey God, to make them rebels against God. Since God had only given them one command to obey, Satan had to zero in on it. What was that command? We find it i nthese verses:

> And the LORD God commanded the man, saying, "Of every tree of the garden you may freely eat; but of the tree of the knowledge of good and evil you shall not eat, for in the day that you eat of it you shall surely die."
> (Gen. 2:16–17)

This is the command that God gave to Adam before Eve was created.

What about this tree? Its name tells us something very important. If Adam and Eve chose to eat of it, they would create for themselves an entirely different kind of existence. They had known only good, but eating of this tree would cause them to know evil along with the good.

This tree was selected by God to give Adam and Eve the opportunity to choose whether they would be faithful to Him. There was nothing in the tree *per se* that made it wrong for them to eat of it. It was wrong because God told them it was wrong. God could have selected a river and told them not to cross it. Or He could have selected a mountain and told them not to climb it. But He chose this tree and told them not to eat of it.

That tree was the test for whether they, as free beings,

would choose obedience to God or disobedience. Satan had chosen disobedience for himself. He hadn't been content to be God's creature and to live under His authority. The issue before Adam and Eve was whether they would make the same choice that Satan had made.

Satan began by planting a doubt in Eve's mind about the goodness of God. He essentially said: "Is what I have heard really true? Is it a fact that God does not allow you to eat of all the trees of the garden?" (v. 1).

The implication was that if God were truly good, He wouldn't have put so much as a single tree off-limits.

Satan proceeded to suggest that God had an ulterior motive in giving them this command, namely, that He was protecting Himself and His position! He knew if Adam and Eve were to eat of that tree, they would be like Him (v. 5)! Lucifer had told himself the lie that he could be like God, and he acted upon it. He now wanted Eve to tell herself the same lie and to act on it.

What Satan Achieved

We know what happened. Eve ate the fruit of the forbidden tree and persuaded Adam to do the same. We might say humanity is still eating of it today. There is so much in our world that is good and wonderful, but there is also an abundance of evil. We see and experience both realities every day.

So this is how Lucifer-turned-Satan brought sin into this world. Frederick S. Leahy describes it in this way:

> Thus man became a rebel against God. He joined forces with Satan. The fall was no mere act of stumbling, but a catastrophe of the first magnitude. In

a moment of time man passed from life to death.[5]
In yet another of his superb works, Leahy writes:

Satan . . . had found a throne on earth: man's heart.[6]

5 Frederick S. Leahy, *Satan Cast Out*, The Banner of Truth Trust, (Edinburgh, UK), 1990, 35.
6 Frederick S. Leahy, *The Victory of the Lamb*, The Banner of Truth Trust (Edinburgh, UK), 2001, 12.

3

Bad News for
the Devil

Please Read:
Genesis 3:15

What did Satan expect to happen when he led Adam and Eve into sin? Did he expect God to walk away from His creatures in humiliating defeat? Did he assume that God would simply leave Adam and Eve to the ravages of sin and death? Did he think God would merely give up in despair and obliterate His creation?

If his thoughts were running along those lines, he would soon learn how very wrong he was. God would neither leave Adam and Eve in their sin nor wipe them out. Three words capture God's response to His sinful, fallen creatures—*pursuing*, *promising*, and *picturing*.

God Pursuing (v. 9)

God came into the garden to seek His creatures, calling out to Adam as He came: "Where are you?" Let it be forever riveted in our minds that Christianity is not about sinners seeking God. Adam and Eve's sin had a devastating effect upon them. It darkened their minds, degraded their affections, and deadened their wills. In other words, it brought spiritual death upon them. Before they sinned, they were alive to God and dead to sin. After they sinned, they were alive to Satan and sin, and dead toward God.

By their disobedience, Adam and Eve had essentially broken their friendship with God and formed a friendship with the devil. Ghastly friendship!

If we truly understand what sin did to Adam and Eve, we will simultaneously understand these words from the apostle Paul:

> There is none righteous, no, not one:
> There is none who understands;
> There is none who seeks after God.
> (Rom. 3:10–11)

Christianity is about God seeking and saving sinners. To talk about sinners seeking God without God first seeking them makes no more sense than talking about a mouse seeking a cat.

God Promising (v. 15)

After finding Adam and Eve, God made a promise. It is the grand and glorious promise of Genesis 3:15, which is often called "the covenant of grace." It was God graciously promising to break the friendship Adam and Eve had established with Satan in order to restore their friendship with Himself. God told Adam and Eve that he was not going to allow their friendship with Satan to stand. He said to the devil:

> I will put enmity
> Between you and the woman. . .

God's first two words, "I will," should fill our hearts with joy. God was announcing that He was shouldering all of the weight of His plan of redemption. Salvation is certainly too big a weight for us to lift! If God hadn't pledged to do all the lifting, there would be no hope for us.

Why did God specify Eve in these words? Why did He say He would put enmity between her and the devil? It may very well be due to the fact that the disobedience of Adam and Eve came about because the devil formed a friendship with Eve. Just as the formation of a friendship with her would inevitably involve Adam, so now the promise of breaking her friendship with Satan would also inevitably involve Adam.

How was God going to break the friendship that Adam and Eve had formed with Satan and return them to friendship with Himself? Genesis 3:15 provides the answer. God's plan was to be accomplished through the "Seed" of the woman.

God wasn't referring to the physical descendants of Eve in general but rather to one descendant in particular—the Lord Jesus Christ.

In effect, then, God was saying to Satan: "You used the man I put here to spoil paradise. I am putting you on notice that I am going to send another Man, another Adam, to undo what you have done. You have succeeded with this Adam, but we will see how you do with the next one."

So we have here the promise of the Second Person of the Trinity, the eternal Son of God, coming to this earth in our humanity.

This promise was fulfilled when Jesus was born. And we should note how the apostle Paul described the coming of Jesus in Galatians 4:4: "But when the fullness of the time had come, God sent forth His Son, born of a woman. . ."

Jesus was indeed the Seed of the woman! He was born of Mary without a human father because He was conceived in her by the Holy Spirit (Matt. 1:20).

Jesus was God's plan to break the friendship of sinners with Satan and make them friends of God again.

And the enmity that God was in the process of creating between His people and Satan certainly existed between Satan and Christ, the Seed of the woman. Oh, how Satan hated the Lord Jesus! How he tempted Him to sin! How he stirred up hatred and animosity toward Him (Heb. 12:3)!

So the coming of Jesus to this earth is promised in Genesis 3:15. But there is more than the incarnation of Jesus here. His crucifixion is also here. It is in these words:

He shall bruise your head,
And you shall bruise His heel.

We must remember that God was speaking here to Satan who had used the serpent to tempt Eve to sin. He promised that His Son, Jesus, would come, and He promised that Satan would hate Him with the utmost hatred.

The hatred Satan had for Jesus would finally culminate in Jesus being crucified. See Him now! There He hangs in agony and blood as Satan and all his minions dance with glee. The One they hate is dying on a cross! They have won the victory—or so it seems!

If Satan and his forces thought the cross was their victory, they grossly miscalculated. Yes, there was real agony and pain on that cross, and, yes, Jesus died there; but all of it amounted to nothing more than Satan inflicting a painful blow to the heel of the Lord Jesus.

The cross was not Satan's victory. It was Jesus' victory. In dying there, the Lord Jesus brought His bruised heel down with crushing force on the head of Satan.

By dying on the cross, the Lord Jesus secured the utter

defeat and final destruction of Satan and his kingdom (Col. 2:13-15).

The hold that Satan has on people is sin. As long as they are in their sins, they are legally his property. But when the penalty for their sins is paid, Satan has to let them go. They are no longer his. The whole purpose of Jesus going to the cross of Calvary was to receive the penalty of sin for all those who believe in Him so Satan no longer has a claim over them. The cross of Christ defeated Satan and destroyed his rule over believers in Christ.

John Stallings got to the heart of the cross in penning these words:

> *See my Jesus on the cross, the people crying.*
> *Looking on, a man would think it tragedy:*
> *But what the world could not see*
> *Was when they nailed Him to that tree,*
> *It would break the chains of sin's captivity.*

God Picturing (v. 21)

After stating the promise of the Redeemer, God killed animals to make coverings for Adam and Eve. In the shedding of the blood of those animals, God was picturing for Adam and Eve that the coming Redeemer would shed His blood to pay for their sin. We can be assured that from that moment, Adam and Eve began to look forward in faith to the coming Christ who would make atonement for sinners by the shedding of His blood.

God has always had only one plan of salvation, and that plan is His Son, Jesus Christ. People in the Old Testament era were saved as they looked forward in faith to the coming Christ. We are saved by looking backward in faith to the Christ who has come. More specifically, all who are saved from sin or ever will be saved have looked or will look to Christ and the blood that He shed on the cross.

No one in heaven will ever ask anyone else how he or she got there for this simple reason—all those in heaven will know that they are there by virtue of the redeeming death of Christ on the cross.

Let's come away from Genesis 3 with a double awe—awe that sin could create such a chasm between God and His creatures, and awe that God in grace could and would cross that chasm.

4

Satan Seeking to Thwart the Promise

Please Read:

Revelation 12:1–6

Some things don't need to be said. We shouldn't be surprised that the third chapter of Genesis doesn't tell us how Satan responded to God's promise to send His Son to redeem sinners. We know how Satan responded. He hated it!

So Satan had to shift his strategy once again. His first strategy was to overthrow God. That didn't work! His second strategy, to get Adam and Eve to rebel against God, *did* work. But when God announced His plan to provide salvation for His fallen creatures, Satan was forced to adopt a new policy, namely, stopping that promise from being fulfilled. What a defeat that would be for God!

To stop God's salvation, Satan had to stop God's Son. Satan knew he would have to succeed in one of two things to stop God's Son. First, he, Satan, would have to keep the Son from coming to this earth. If he failed in that, he would have to turn his attention to keeping the Lord Jesus from doing the work that He would come to do.

The first of these two strategies is put before us in picturesque fashion in Revelation 12:1–6. Here we meet a woman, a child, and a dragon.

The woman should be regarded as a symbol of God's people in the Old Testament era. The allusions to the sun, moon, and stars represent the radiance and glory of the people of God.

The woman is pictured as pregnant, and she cries in anguish until she gives birth to her child. This cry of travail fills the Old Testament as the people of God yearn for the coming of "the Seed of the woman" (Gen. 3:15).

The Child is the Lord Jesus Christ, who is destined to rule the nations with a rod of iron (Ps. 2:9; Rev. 2:27; 19:15). He came to the people of God who were "pregnant" with the promise of the Messiah.

The dragon is Satan himself. The fact that he was standing in front of the woman to devour her child conveys all his schemes to keep Jesus from coming to this earth. So the Old Testament era was one of expectancy and resistance, with God's people doing the expecting and Satan doing the resisting.

At this point, we must consider God's focusing of His promise to send the Messiah. The Messiah would have to be born in a particular nation. So God selected Abraham to be the father of the nation of Israel and promised that the Messiah would come to that nation (Acts 3:25–26).

The Messiah would also have to be born into a family. So God chose the family of David (2 Sam. 7:16; Ps. 89:35–37).

We should expect the Old Testament to tell us about the devil's schemes to destroy both the nation of Israel and the house of David. And it does. If there was no nation of Israel or no house of David, there could be no Messiah.

Satan Seeking to Destroy Israel

One of the devil's attempts to destroy Israel came when the descendants of Jacob were forced by famine to move to Egypt. They lived there in peace for a while, but then a new Pharaoh came along and subjected the Israelites to oppressive slavery. At one point, this Pharaoh ordered all newborn Israelite males to be killed (Ex. 1:15–22).

This decree from Pharaoh might seem to be nothing more than a king employing a political strategy to maintain his own power. But behind Pharaoh's decision was Satan himself.

Imagine now that we have hurled ourselves through the centuries and landed in Egypt toward the end of the Israelites' long bondage there (430 years). Suppose someone asked us during our visit to offer an assessment of whether the nation of Israel could survive. We would be quick to say it couldn't.

But it did. Being fully aware of what Satan was attempting to do, God protected His people while they were in Egypt and eventually delivered them in miraculous ways from their bondage.

Frederick Leahy summarizes it well: "Thus God overruled the Satanic assault on Israel directed by Pharaoh . . . . The Messianic line stood firm."[7]

Another of Satan's attempts to destroy Israel occurred when the nation was carried into captivity in Babylon. Many would have regarded this as the end of Israel, but God again intervened and delivered them.

Satan Seeking to Destroy the House of David

Another of Satan's attempts to destroy the Messianic promise is described in 2 Kings 11 and in 2 Chronicles 22 and 23. These chapters introduce us to Queen Athaliah, one of the most despicable people to ever walk across the human stage.

This Athaliah was the daughter of Ahab. Her father, a disgusting specimen himself, brought the worship of Baal into Israel to an unprecedented level. Athaliah, also

7 Leahy, *The Victory of the Lamb*, 30.

a devoted worshiper of Baal, married Jehoram, king of Judah. (The nation of Israel was now divided into two kingdoms—one taking the name of Judah, the other retaining the name of Israel.) When Athaliah's husband and her son—both descendants of David—died, Athaliah took the throne of Judah. There was no doubt in her mind about her first order of business. She immediately set out to "destroy all the royal heirs" (2 Kings 11:1).

All the royal heirs in Judah were descendants of David, Athaliah's plan, then, was to destroy all of David's house so he would have no more descendants. We should see Satan's fingerprints all over this deal. The house of David was the house from which the Messiah would come (2 Sam. 7:12–16). If David's family was completely wiped out, God's promise could not have been fulfilled.

Athaliah almost pulled it off. She succeeded in eliminating all of David's descendants except for one child, Joash. She would have eliminated him as well if she had known about him, but the priest Jehoiada and his wife, Jehosheba, hid the boy for six years. When he reached the age of seven, they succeeded in getting him crowned as king and in having Athaliah executed.

One little boy! It would seem as if the plan of God was hanging by a very slender thread and that thread was about to snap! But God's threads are very strong and can't be snapped! Satan was pulling Athaliah's strings. Her scheme was his scheme. But the scheme failed, and the house of David survived.

Satan Seeking to Destroy the Baby Jesus

God's promise to send the Messiah put Satan to work, and work he did with scheme after scheme to derail the promise. Each of them came to naught. Scheme after scheme met with failure after failure. But Satan is nothing if not persistent. The long-awaited time finally arrived. Joseph and Mary had made their way to Bethlehem, and Jesus was born. Did Satan concede defeat? Not for a moment! When Jesus was born, the dragon was still seeking to devour the child. This time his weapon of choice was King Herod of Israel.

Matthew's Gospel provides the account. Having seen a special star and having calculated from that star that a king had been born in Israel, wise men from the East came to Herod with this question: "Where is He who has been born King of the Jews?" (Matt. 2:3). That set off all of Herod's alarm bells! A king born in Israel? Herod would tolerate no rival! He would determine the precise location of this newborn king and eliminate Him! When that effort proved futile, this vile and reprehensible man ordered the execution of all male children in the Bethlehem area who were two years of age and under (Matt. 2:3–18).

It was Satan who prompted and directed this whole affair. It was yet another of his plans, and it turned out to be another of his defeats. God warned the wise men not to report to Herod that they had found the child (Matt. 2:12), and He directed Joseph to flee to Egypt with Mary and the baby (Matt. 2:13–15). Satan's devouring was diverted by God's devising.

Jesus had arrived. The promise had been fulfilled. Satan had been defeated. The only policy remaining for him was to seek to prevent Jesus from accomplishing His mission. More about that in a later chapter!

Part II—
The Evil Empire

5

The Reality of Demons

Please Read:
1 John 5:19; Revelation 12:7–12

We have been focusing on Satan, the master demon. We recall that he was originally Lucifer, and we recall that he, filled with himself, attempted to overthrow God. One third of all the angels joined him in this effort. The result was that Lucifer and all of his allies were cast out of heaven.

What happened to all of the angels who took Lucifer's side? Did they merely cease to exist? No. These fallen angels now make up Satan's evil empire. They are at work to advance his agenda on this earth. The Bible commonly refers to them as demons, but it also refers to them as evil spirits or unclean spirits. Because demons were originally angels, they have, in the words of Joel Beeke, the "essential properties" of angels. He writes:

> Demons are immaterial, invisible, asexual, and immortal spirits. They are intelligent, affectionate, and morally responsible beings made to serve God. They are organized, swift, powerful, and fearsome beings. Yet they were created by God, and are local and limited, not omnipresent, omniscient, or omnipotent.[8]

8 Joel R. Beeke and Paul M. Smalley, *Reformed Systematic Theology*, (Wheaton, IL), Crossway, 2019, vol. i, 1137.

But are they real, or are they mere figments of overactive imaginations? To put it another way, why should we believe that demons actually exist?

The Old Testament Affirms the Reality of Demons

The Old Testament often condemns practices that are commonly associated with demons. God specifically warned the Israelites to be on guard against "mediums" and those with "familiar spirits" (Lev. 19:31; 20:6). It also warns against witchcraft, soothsaying, sorcery, interpretations of omens, spiritism, and calling up the dead (Deut. 18:9–14). Through the prophet Isaiah, the Lord warns His people about "mediums," "wizards," "charmers," and "sorcerers" (Isa. 8:19; 19:3).

Leviticus 17:7 and Deuteronomy 32:17 equate idolatry with sacrificing to demons, as does Psalm 106:37.

The New King James Version identifies the spirit that troubled Saul as "a distressing spirit," and the King James Version calls it "an evil spirit." The fact that it was sent by the Lord means that He judged Saul for his sinfulness by allowing the demon to trouble him (1 Sam. 16:14–16; 18:10; 19:9). This same king, in a flagrant violation of God's laws, consulted a witch to bring Samuel the prophet up from the dead (1 Sam. 28:3–25).

King Jeroboam of Israel rejected the priests appointed by the Lord and put in their place "priests . . . for the demons" (2 Chron. 11:15).

King Ahab of Israel was deceived by "a lying spirit" (1 Kings 22:19–23), and Manasseh, king of Judah, was so devoted to cultic and demonic practices that he sacrificed his own son to an idol (2 Kings 21:6).

One of Job's three friends, Eliphaz, was visited by a spirit who denied that it is possible for mere mortals to be right with God (Job 4:12–21).

In Psalm 106 we find a sad summary of the history of the nation of Israel. Verse 37 says:

> They even sacrificed their sons
> And their daughters to demons, . . .

The Lord Jesus Affirmed the Reality of Demons

While the testimony of the Old Testament to the reality of demons is frequent and convincing, it is the testimony of Jesus that is truly decisive for believers. Each person who professes faith in Christ and yet doubts the existence of demons should ask himself or herself this question: How can I call Jesus "Lord" and doubt what He says about demons?

The Lord Jesus both spoke about demons and cast out demons. We will deal with the latter in a later chapter. For now, we focus on what Jesus said about demons.

When Jesus sent His twelve disciples on a preaching mission, He explicitly told them to "cast out demons" (Matt. 10:8).

Then there was that time that the Pharisees accused Jesus of casting out demons by using the power and authority of Beelzebub, the ruler of the demons, and Jesus showed the utter absurdity of their argument. On one hand, He said: ". . . if Satan casts out Satan, he is divided against himself. How then will his kingdom stand?" (Matt. 12:26). On the other hand, He said: "But if I cast out demons by the Spirit of God, surely the kingdom of God has come upon you" (Matt. 12:27).

A bit later, Jesus spoke about "an unclean spirit" going out of a man only to return to that same man with "seven other spirits more wicked than himself" (Matt. 12:43–45).

It's obvious that Jesus had absolutely no hesitation to say that demons are real and formidable foes. Some people dismiss this by saying Jesus was merely speaking as a man of the times in which He lived. In those times, people believed in demons, so Jesus believed in demons. If Jesus were physically present in our times of scientific and intellectual sophistication, He would know demons don't exist. But this reduces Jesus to being nothing more than an ordinary man and flies in the face of Scripture's fundamental teaching that He was (and is) the God-man. He was fully God and fully man, making Him utterly unique and putting Him in a totally different category than "a man of His times."

The argument that Jesus was mistaken about demons because He was "a man of His time" opens this question: What else was Jesus mistaken about? To go down this road of Jesus being mistaken even for a short distance will finally and inevitably lead us to say we can't trust Jesus at all on anything.

The Leaders of the Early Church Affirmed the Reality of Demons

In addition to the testimony of the Old Testament and the testimony of Jesus, we can add that of the leaders of the early church. In his letter to the Ephesians, the apostle Paul identifies demons as "principalities," "powers," "the rulers of darkness," and "spiritual hosts of wickedness" (Eph. 6:12).

Another apostle, John, urged his readers to "not believe every spirit," but rather "test the spirits" to determine "whether they are of God" (1 John 4:1). He further tells them that those spirits who deny the truth about Jesus have "the spirit of the Antichrist" (1 John 4:3).

In the book of Revelation, the apostle John relates a vision in which he saw "three unclean spirits like frogs coming out of the mouth of the dragon" (Rev. 16:13). John doesn't leave us in doubt about these "unclean spirits." He says they are "spirits of demons" (Rev. 16:14).

The author of the epistle of James was the half-brother of Jesus. He declared the reality of demons in these words: "You believe that there is one God. You do well. Even the demons believe—and tremble!" (James 2:19).

The physician Luke, who wrote the book of Acts, relates Philip preaching in the city of Samaria. One result of his ministry there was that "unclean spirits, crying with a loud voice, came out of many who were possessed; . . ." (Acts 8:5–7). Luke also recounts the apostle Paul casting the demon out of a slave girl (Acts 16:16–18). He likewise includes the account of the ill-fated attempt of the seven sons of Sceva to cast a demon out of a man. The evil spirit spoke these words to them: "Jesus I know, and Paul I know; but who are you?" Then the possessed man "leaped on them, overpowered them, and prevailed against them, so that they fled out of that house naked and wounded" (Acts 19:11–20).

Some will object to these evidences for the existence of demons with these words: "All of these come from the Bible. How can we know the Bible is true?" For the answer to that question, please see chapter fourteen.

6

The Activities
of Demons

Please Read:
2 Corinthians 2:11

D emons despise idleness. Driven by intense hatred for God and His people, the demons are always active. Given the fact that there are many demons, perhaps even millions, that constitutes a lot of activity.

But what do demons do? Yes, they oppose God and the people of God, but how do they conduct that opposition? Before Jesus came, they attempted to keep Him from coming. After He came, they sought to keep Him from carrying out His mission. Having failed in those two objectives, they now focus their attention on people in general and on God's people in particular. Three words seem to capture most of their efforts—deception, persecution, and possession.

Deception

The demons delight in deception. In the next chapter, we will go into more detail about one kind of deception, namely, apostasy. Our concern at this point is the deception the demons practice to keep unbelievers from coming to faith.

The devil loves lies and falsehood. The Lord Jesus made this clear. Speaking of the devil, He said that he "does not stand in the truth, because there is no truth in him. When he speaks a lie, he speaks from his own resources, for he is a liar and the father of it" (John 8:44b).

If the devil loves lies and falsehood, we can be sure that his demons do as well. To love falsehood is to hate truth; Satan and his forces are haters of the truth. They hate the truth because the truth sets people free (John 8:32). The truth of the gospel frees sinners from their sins. The gospel is the good news of Jesus providing for sinners the righteousness they don't have and paying the penalty for the sins they do have. It snaps the chains of Satan and sin and brings them into "the glorious liberty of the children of God" (Rom. 8:21). Jesus put it in these wonderful words: "Therefore if the Son makes you free, you shall be free indeed" (John 8:36).

The satanic forces don't want people to be free. They want them forever shackled in sin. So they practice deception. Jesus highlighted this kind of deception in His parable of the sower. He noted that some of the seed sown "fell by the wayside" (Luke 8:5). He later offered this explanation: "The seed is the word of God. Those by the wayside are the ones who hear; then the devil comes and takes away the word out of their hearts, lest they should believe and be saved" (Luke 8:11b–12).

The apostle Paul struck this same note when he said unbelievers have their minds "blinded" by "the god of this age" so that the light of the gospel will not shine on them (2 Cor. 4:4).

The demons of hell have no shortage of ways to keep people from believing in Christ. The unbeliever is in the pew. The preacher steps up to the pulpit to proclaim the glorious gospel of Jesus Christ. The battle is joined. The unbeliever finds himself thinking about all he has to do in the coming week. He is distracted by the fidgety person in the pew nearby. He sees someone that he knows is a member of the church, but he also knows that person makes no attempt to live as a Christian should. He remembers his college professors ridiculing Christianity as a crutch for the weak-minded. The preacher mentions the Bible, but the man remembers how his professors had assured him that no intelligent person could believe in such an old book. The preacher talks about sin, death, and hell, and points people to Christ, but Mr. Unbeliever recalls reading a survey that indicated that very few modern people believe in such things. The sermon ends, the service concludes, and the unbeliever walks out, not for a moment suspecting that he has been targeted by demons who are bent on his destruction. He tells his friends that he went to church. They laugh and assure him that he was fed a pack of lies. Indeed, he was—but the pack of lies came not from the pulpit but from the pit—the pit of hell!

Is there any hope for someone who is kept in unbelief by the deception of the devil? There is! It is found in these words from the apostle Paul: " . . . God perhaps will grant them repentance, so that they may know the truth, and that they may come to their senses and escape the snare of the devil, having been taken captive by him to do his will" (2 Tim. 2:25b–26).

Persecution

When the demons can't keep people from coming to faith in Christ, they try to make them sorry that they did. To that end, they stir up people to persecute Christians. This can happen on a small scale—an individual unbeliever persecuting an individual believer—or it can happen on a large scale. But whatever the scale, the devil and his demons are behind it. Persecution is evil, and evil comes from the devil and his forces.

The history of persecution is long. It began shortly after the fall of Adam and Eve. God's promise in Genesis 3:15 plainly declares a fundamental division in the human race between those who belong to Satan and those who belong to God. It wouldn't be long until Adam and Eve saw that division in action when their eldest son, Cain, killed his brother Abel.

Noah encountered severe ridicule and scorn as he acted upon God's warning of a coming flood and began building the ark.

The people of Israel were enslaved for centuries in Egypt. David was persecuted by King Saul, as was Elijah by King Ahab. Daniel was thrown into a lions' den. Jesus was hated, persecuted, and crucified. Peter and John were jailed. Stephen was stoned, James was executed, and Paul was whipped, beaten, stoned, imprisoned, and beheaded. And these are just a few of the peaks in the long mountain range of persecution.

It must be said again—all of this was the devil's handiwork.

The supreme irony of it all is that it fulfills these words from Jesus to His disciples: "Remember the word that I said to you, 'A servant is not greater than his master.' If they persecuted Me, they will also persecute you" (John 15:20a).

But the persecution that has always been present for God's people will be greatly intensified toward the end, and that intensification will be engineered by Satan himself. The book of Revelation lays this out for us. The dragon (Rev. 12:1–17), the beast out of the sea (Rev. 13:1–10), and the beast out of the earth (Rev. 13:11–18) will spearhead this persecution. The dragon is Satan, the sea-born beast represents anti-Christian government, and the earth-born beast represents anti-Christian religion.

So the devil-devised, devil-driven, devil-delighting persecution that has gone on through the centuries will come to a mighty crescendo at the end of time. But it will all come to nothing. It won't topple God from His throne, and it won't keep one Christian from being richly rewarded in heaven.

Possession

Demons deceive and persecute, but they also possess people. When Jesus was engaged in His earthly ministry, there seemed to be an unusual outbreak of demon possession, but it's safe to say that there has never been an era in which there has been no demon possession. As noted in the previous section, the end of time will feature another tremendous outbreak of demon activity, which, of course, will include demon possession.

We understand why some individuals are demon-possessed. They actually seek it. They are obsessed with the satanic, and they are rewarded accordingly.

But there is also involuntary possession. A demon or demons simply target someone and possess him or her. How they choose their involuntary targets isn't completely clear, but people who delight in sinful behavior and couple that with extreme hardness toward the things of God can unwittingly put out the welcome mat for demon possession.

Having said these things, we have to admit that there are cases of demon possession that fall outside our ability to explain. We think of the boy described in Luke 9 and the slave girl in Acts 16. How did their demons take possession of them?

This doesn't mean that all without exception can be

demon-possessed. True Christians are safe. Frederick S. Leahy puts it neatly: "Satan cannot recapture the man who is kept by Christ."[9]

He further says: "The unbelieving world is in Satan's embrace, but the Christian is in the arms of the Saviour."[10]

9 Leahy, *Satan Cast Out*, 175.
10 Ibid.

7

Demons and Apostasy

Please Read:
1 Timothy 4:1–3

D emons never lack ways to fight God and His people. One of the many weapons that they have in their arsenal is apostasy. Apostasy is an ugly word. It means "falling away." The apostate is one who "falls away" from the truth. This means that he or she held to the truth for a while, but didn't continue with it.

While the word "apostasy" doesn't appear in the Bible, the reality of it certainly does appear. The apostle Paul says "some will depart from the faith" (1 Tim. 4:1). In 2 Thessalonians 2:3, he mentions "the falling away." He further places Hymenaeus, Philetus, and Demas in the category of apostasy (2 Tim. 2:17–18; 4:10).

The apostle John refers to "those who went out from us" (1 John 2:19). Jude makes mention of some who "crept in unnoticed" while they were actually deniers of "the only Lord God and our Lord Jesus Christ" (Jude 4). The author of Hebrews mentions those who "fall away" (Heb. 6:6) and those who "draw back" (Heb. 10:39). And Jesus told His disciples that at the end of time "the love of many will grow cold," and He added: "But He who endures to the end shall be saved" (Matt. 24:12–13).

Other Scriptures could be cited as well, but the ones we have noted make the point in loud and clear fashion— apostasy is real.

Why the Devil and His Demons Promote Apostasy

The devil and his forces fervently desire to discredit Christianity, and apostasy does that. Here is a person who has made a profession of faith in Christ and been baptized. He has joined the church, and he becomes very active in the church. He very seldom misses a service, and he begins to hold various offices in the church. Then one day he walks away from it all. The church members are befuddled. They contact him again and again to persuade him to return, but he rebuffs their invitations, kindly at first, but then with a curtness and belligerence. He insists that he "no longer believes in that stuff."

It isn't hard to see why this situation brings great joy to the demons. It discredits the church in the eyes of the community. The comment is often made that this particular man tried Christianity, but it didn't work. And the demons rejoice in it because it brings discouragement to those who are still in the church.

So the assumption that the devil never wants anyone to join a church is wrong. He and his minions are very happy when unconverted people join Bible-believing, gospel-preaching churches. And, yes, that's the problem with apostates. They have never truly come to Christ in saving faith. The apostle John puts it powerfully: "They went out from us, but they were not of us; for if they had been of us, they would have continued with us; but they went out that they might be made manifest, that none of them were of us" (1 John 2:19).

Not all of who fall away from biblical churches are apostates. Some are backsliders who, after a time, return to the Lord and His work. The apostate is one who departs with an attitude of finality and hostility.

How the Devil and His Demons Promote Apostasy

The devil does most of his work by trickery and deceit. It's no different with his work of apostasy. The apostle Paul writes: "Now the Spirit expressly says that in latter times some will depart from the faith, giving heed to deceiving spirits and doctrines of demons, . . ." (1 Tim. 4:1).

"Deceiving spirits" are behind apostasy, and they have their own doctrines. It's not hard to identify these doctrines. They are anti-doctrines, that is, they are the opposite of all the major doctrines of the Bible. Does the Bible teach the sinful depravity of men and women and in need of the Savior? The demons say human beings are basically good and need no redemption. Does the Bible affirm that Jesus lived sinlessly? The demons say He didn't. Does the Bible tell us that Jesus died as a substitute for sinners, actually bearing the wrath of God in their stead so they never have to bear it themselves? The demons deny it. Does the Bible tell us that Jesus arose from the grave? The demons say that His resurrection is nothing but a hoax. Does the Bible promise that Jesus is coming again? The demons laugh as they cry: "Where is the promise of His coming?" (2 Peter 3:4).

The demons challenge these doctrines in a deceptive, seductive manner. They point to the most and the best. They observe that most people don't believe in the doctrines of the gospel and ask: "How could so many be wrong?" They also call attention to those that they regard as the best of society—the celebrities, the members of academia, the political leaders—and they ask: "How could such intelligent, important people be wrong?

The demons have often lured people away from the Christian faith by putting before them very highly educated, personable, entertaining ministers who deny the faith (2 Cor. 11:13–15). False ministers come into the church acting very sweetly, but they prove in the end to have acted very savagely (Acts 20:28–30).

Knowing the wiles of the devil, as he most certainly did, the apostle Paul wrote to the believers in Corinth: "But I fear, lest somehow, as the serpent deceived Eve by his craftiness, so your minds may be corrupted from the simplicity that is in Christ" (2 Cor. 11:3),

By "the simplicity that is in Christ," Paul was denoting the pure, unadulterated gospel of Christ. Hating it as they do, the demons are very devoted to adulterating it.

What the Devil and His Demons Will Do to Promote Apostasy in the Future

The demonic forces have made sure that we have had apostasy all along the way. There has never been an era without it. It revealed itself very early in human history with Cain, the first son of Adam and Eve, rejecting God's way of redemption. It has been with us ever since.

But Satan's army will unveil a special kind of apostasy at the end of time. That is "the falling away" that Paul mentions in 2 Thessalonians 2:3. It will occur in conjunction with the appearance of the Antichrist (2 Thess. 2:1–12).

As the gospel age draws to a close, there will be great numbers of people who will apostatize. Many will abandon the outward appearance of Christianity and will become very hostile toward it. They will proudly count themselves among those who never embraced Christianity but rather have been opposed to it all along. They will gladly accept the mark of the beast on their foreheads and right hands, that is, they will happily think and do as the Antichrist will have them to think and do. Fueled by an intense desire to be considered intelligent and driven by a fervent yearning to enjoy the pleasures this world offers, many will not only turn away *from* Christianity but also will turn *against* it.

The demons' promotion of apostasy is bad news. The good news is that no one who has truly come to faith in Christ will ever fall away from it. The Christian can become cold and careless in his walk with the Lord, but he or she will never apostatize. To put it another way, the true Christian may often fall on the deck of the ship, but he or she will never fall overboard.

Apostasy is not falling away from the *possession* of the Christian faith. It is rather falling away from the *profession* of the Christian faith. What the author of Hebrews said to his original readers can equally well be said to all believers today: "But we are not of those who draw back to perdition, but of those who believe to the saving of the soul" (Heb. 10:39).

Part III—
Jesus and the
Demons

8

Satan
Tempting Jesus

Please Read:

Matthew 4:1–11

M any centuries have come and gone since God made the promise of Genesis 3:15. The Seed of the woman came as promised. His name was Jesus. Satan tried to kill Him shortly after He was born, but God thwarted that scheme. Jesus has now grown into adulthood. Having been baptized by John the Baptist, He is about to launch His public ministry. Before He does so, He goes into the wilderness for forty days. This was not a mistake or miscalculation on His part. It wasn't a poor choice. The Gospel accounts make it clear that Jesus went there to engage and defeat Satan (Matt. 4:1; Mark 1:12; Luke 4:1). From the moment God promised to Satan that He would send His Son, it was a given that the two would eventually meet. That hour has arrived.

It's difficult for us to know how much Satan knew. We know that Satan isn't omniscient. God alone possesses that quality. We wonder how much Satan knew in his limited knowledge. We can be sure that he knew that Jesus came to this earth as the Second Adam. Yielding to Satan's tempting, the first Adam had plunged the human race into sin and condemnation. As the Second Adam, Jesus was throwing the gauntlet down. He was challenging Satan to repeat with Him, the new Adam, the victory that he had won over the first Adam. So Satan came to Jesus in the wilderness determined to derail and defeat Jesus.

Jesus' circumstances were a far cry from Adam's. Jesus was in a barren wilderness, while Adam was in a beautiful garden. Jesus was hungry, having fasted for forty days. Adam, being free to eat of all the trees of Eden except one, was well fed. Jesus was alone except for the companionship of wild beasts (Mark 1:13). Adam was not alone, having been given Eve as his companion.

The Messianic Tasks

To understand the temptations Jesus faced, we must place them in the context of His messiahship which required three major things of Him.

FIRST, He had to take to Himself our humanity. In order to *do* something for us, He had to *be* one of us.

SECOND, He had to live in perfect obedience to God, doing all that He commanded and refusing to do anything He had not commanded. If Jesus had committed so much as a single sin, He would have made Himself a sinner in need of a Savior. If He had put Himself in the position of needing a Savior, He would have disqualified Himself from being the Savior.

THIRD, He had to die on the cross, and, in so doing, secure a kingdom for Himself. This kingdom would be spiritual in nature and consist of all those whom He came to save (John 18:36–37).

The Satanic Temptations

The temptations that Satan employed against Jesus were all designed to get Him to misuse His messiahship. A misused messiahship was no messiahship at all, and no messiahship would mean no salvation for sinners.

Satan FIRST tempted Jesus, who was famished after

fasting for forty days, to turn stones into bread (vv. 3–4). Had Jesus yielded to this temptation, He would have denied the humanity that He took when He came to this earth. Mere men don't turn stones into bread. If Jesus came to this earth to live as a man, He had to live as a man. He couldn't temporarily set His humanity aside to meet His needs.

The SECOND temptation was for Jesus to leap off the pinnacle of the temple (vv. 5–7), and, in so doing, prove that He was indeed God's Son. Had Jesus done this, He would have violated the second of His messianic tasks, which was to live in perfect obedience to God. This leap would have had Him doing something that God hadn't commanded. It was something that wasn't on the Father's agenda for Him, and He, Jesus, came to always please the Father (John 8:29).

The THIRD temptation, to secure for Himself a kingdom by worshiping Satan, would have violated the third of His messianic tasks. That task was to secure a special kingdom for Himself by dying on the cross. So with this temptation, Satan was seeking to divert Jesus from the cross. It was Satan's call for Jesus to secure the end—a kingdom—without using the means that the Father had appointed.

The Terrific Triumph

Although everything seemed to be stacked against Jesus having success against Satan, the outcome wasn't in doubt. We should never view these temptations as tests to see if Jesus would sin, but rather as opportunities for Him to prove that He wouldn't sin. When a tire manufacturer hoists a truck in the air and drops it to the ground, it isn't to see if the tires will blow out, but rather to prove that they won't. Jesus wasn't about to "blow out," but Satan seems to have nurtured the hope that He would.

Jesus emerged from the battle with His messiahship intact. That's the good news. The bad news is this: the fact that Satan couldn't defeat Jesus doesn't mean that he has gone out of the tempting business. Now he focuses his attention of Jesus' followers. We must always be aware of his desire to trip us up, and we need to realize that he is a very subtle and clever foe (2 Cor. 11:3; 1 Peter 5:8). Jesus is our example for defeating him. He fended off each of Satan's temptations by resorting to Scripture, and we should do the same. The more we feed our minds on the Word of God, the more strength we will have to stand against Satan.

O loving wisdom of our God!
When all was sin and shame;
A second Adam to the fight
And to the rescue came.

O wisest love! that flesh and blood,
That did in Adam fail,
Should strive afresh against the foe,
Should strive and should prevail!

(John Henry Newman)

9

Jesus' Authority over the Demons

Please Read:

Mark 5:1–20

The Gospels of Matthew, Mark, and Luke make much of Jesus casting out demons. Mark and Luke describe Him going into the synagogue in Capernaum. Confronted there by a man with "an unclean spirit," He immediately rebuked the spirit and cast him out of the man (Mark 1:21–28; Luke 4:31–37). In Matthew and Luke, we find accounts of Jesus delivering a mute man who was demon-possessed (Matt. 9:32–34; Luke 11:14–15). Matthew also includes the account of Jesus casting the demon out of a man who was both blind and mute (Matt. 12:22–23). Still further, Matthew and Mark present Jesus casting a demon out of a Canaanite woman's daughter (Matt. 15:22–28; Mark 7:24–30) and Luke joins them in relating the story of Jesus casting a demon out of a young boy (Matt. 17:14–21; Mark 9:14–29; Luke 9:37–42). Mark and Luke inform us that Jesus cast seven demons out of Mary Magdalene (Mark 16:9; Luke 8:2).

In addition to these accounts of Jesus casting demons out of various individuals, we find this general statement from Mark regarding Jesus: "Then He healed many who were sick with various diseases, and cast out many demons; and He did not allow the demons to speak because they knew Him" (Mark 1:34). Similar statements are found in Mark 3:10–11 and Luke 4:40–41.

We should note that Mark and Luke distinguish

between those who were sick and those who were demon-possessed. Those who explain demon-possession as ancient people attributing sickness to demon-possession should pay attention to Mark and Luke. Sickness was one thing; demon-possession was another.

The testimony of these Gospels is plain. Jesus had incontestable authority over demons, and He exercised it on a very wide scale.

A Great Challenge to Jesus' Authority

To demonstrate the authority of Jesus over demons, we must go to the supreme example of it, namely, His casting the demons out of a man in the country of the Gadarenes, which was located on "the other side of the sea" (Mark 5:1), that is, the Sea of Galilee. Matthew and Mark give an account of this (Matt. 8:28–34; Mark 5:1–20), but we immediately notice a problem! Matthew mentions two demon-possessed men and Mark only one. Those who are eager to discredit the Bible quickly seize on this. As far as they are concerned, it is a glaring contradiction. It would be if Mark had said there was *only* one demoniac, but he said no such thing. He obviously chose to focus on the more prominent and ferocious of the two men that Jesus delivered on that day.

Why should we regard Jesus' dealings with this particular demoniac as the supreme example of His authority over demons? For one thing, this man was possessed by many demons. The demon who spoke to Jesus said: "My name is Legion; for we are many" (Mark 5:9). A Roman legion consisted of 6,000 soldiers. That's a lot of demons!

This multi-possessed man gives us insight into some of the ways that demon-possession can manifest itself.

For one thing, he had superhuman strength. The citizens of that area had tried to bind him, but he easily snapped their chains and shackles (vv. 3-4).

Then there was the extreme mental anguish evidenced by this man constantly crying out and cutting himself with stones (v. 5).

So the demons gave their poor victim both great power and great pain.

Demon-possession also manifests itself in the victim speaking with a voice that isn't his own. In this situation, one demon spoke for all the other demons, and the man himself didn't speak.

It is interesting that the demoniac recognized Jesus from afar and "ran and worshiped Him" (v. 6). While Satan is a powerful foe, he knows that he is not more powerful than God, and Jesus was and is God. The devil also knows that he is destined to experience eternal torment. Here he expresses the fear that Jesus had come to implement that torment (v. 7).

The fact that Satan knew the truth about Jesus and about eternal torment means that he is a better theologian than the professors and pastors who question these things.

Jesus' Great Response to the Great Challenge

Knowing that Jesus was going to drive them out of the man, the demons began to beg Him to not send them "out of the country" but into a nearby herd of pigs (vv. 10-12).

Why did the demons desire to go into the pigs? They may very well have feared, as noted above, that Jesus had come to cast them into hell. Or, as some believe, it was because they are disembodied spirits, and, as such, desire to possess some kind of body. Knowing Jesus would not let them possess another human being, they concluded that the pigs were the next best option!

It is also possible that Satan is here resorting to a kind of Plan B. He is never without plans! If Jesus allowed his demons to go into the pigs, perhaps Satan felt sure that the Gadarenes would turn against Jesus, and he, Satan, would be able to keep his grip on that area.

Jesus' consent to the demons' request has confounded and mystified many. Why did He sanction the destruction of 2,000 animals when He could have driven the demons away without it? Some who have bacon or sausage for breakfast and pork chops for supper wring their hands over this and conclude that Jesus cares nothing for animals!

So what can we say about Jesus' reasons for complying with the demons' plea? One answer is that, in doing so, He gave a powerful and vivid picture of Satan's power to destroy and of His own power to deliver. How people today, especially young people, need to learn that Satan is a destroyer! He does not bring happiness; he ruins it. And how people need to learn that Jesus alone can deliver us from the tyranny of Satan!

Another answer is that Jesus was setting the stage for the Gadarenes to make a choice. Would those people prize their pigs or would they prize Jesus?

With the demon-possessed man sitting before them in perfect peace and tranquility, and with their pigs in the sea, the Gadarenes made their choice. The loss of their pigs touched them far more deeply than the deliverance of the man who had posed such a threat to their community. They would rather have their pigs and terror than have Jesus and peace. So they "began to plead with Him to depart from their region'" (v. 17).

Many repeat the error of the Gadarenes, choosing to

have sin and all the hurt it produces rather than choosing to have Christ.

Jesus did depart, but, in kindness that those citizens did not deserve, He left as His witness the man whom He had delivered (vv. 18–20).

The drama reported in Mark's account of this miracle is still being played out. Satan is still destroying, Jesus is still delivering, and many people are still preferring Satan over Jesus. This drama will continue until the end. At that time, the same Jesus who won the victory over Satan at Gadara will win the final victory over him (Rev. 20:10), and those who spent their lives preferring Satan will share his doom (Matt. 25:41).

10

Jesus Binding Satan

Please Read:
Revelation 20:1–3

L ots and lots of Christians would be quick to say: "If there is anything I know about Satan, it is that he isn't bound."

That indeed seems to be the case. This world is awash with war, crime, political corruption, sexual immorality, deceitfulness, hatred, and anger. Homes are falling apart, churches are declining, civility is disappearing, and paganism is advancing. All of these things and more are Satan's handiwork. So it seems as if he is having himself a field day, and to suggest that he is bound is to brand oneself as a lunatic.

Is the Bible with us when we say Satan isn't bound? Or does it say otherwise?

The Testimony of the Gospels

In Matthew 12:23–30, we have the account of Jesus delivering a man who had been rendered blind and mute by a demon. The Pharisees, who hated Jesus, came up with the ludicrous argument that Jesus was using the power of the devil to cast out the devil. Jesus answered in this way: "And if Satan casts out Satan, he is divided against himself. How then will his kingdom stand?" (v. 26). Jesus then gave them the true explanation for what He had done. He told them that He had entered the strong man's house and plundered his goods. The strong man was, of course, Satan himself. Jesus put it in these words: " . . . how can one enter a strong man's house and plunder his goods, unless he first binds the strong man? And then he will plunder his house" (v. 29).

Jesus was quite obviously declaring that His work of binding Satan had already begun.

When Jesus sent out seventy missionaries, they returned saying: "Lord, even the demons are subject to us in Your name." Jesus responded: "I saw Satan fall like lightning from heaven" (Luke 10:17–18).

In John 12:27–36, Jesus spoke about His forthcoming death on the cross. He included these words: "Now is the judgment of this world; now the ruler of this world will be cast out" (v. 31).

The references to the binding, falling, and casting out of Satan are equivalent. They all refer to Satan being defeated, and they are all connected with the first coming of Jesus.

The Testimony of Paul

In Colossians 2:14 and 15, the apostle rejoiced in what the Lord Jesus Christ accomplished when He was "nailed to the cross" (v. 14). What did Jesus accomplish on that cross? Paul writes: "Having disarmed principalities and powers, He made a public spectacle of them, triumphing over them in it" (v. 15).

The "it" is, of course, the cross on which Jesus died. Paul was assuring his readers that the Lord Jesus had won a complete and decisive victory over the forces of hell by means of His death. When Jesus was crucified, He defeated the whole empire of evil. There He "disarmed principalities and powers," making "a public spectacle of them" and "triumphing" over them.

On the cross, the Lord Jesus stripped the weapons from the hands of all demonic powers and made all of those powers His captives. As far as mere outward appearances were concerned, the cross looked as if it were a great defeat for Jesus. In reality, it was triumph for Him and defeat for Satan. It was actually Jesus leading Satan and all the forces of hell in a victory parade. The biggest thing that ever happened in this dark world occurred when Jesus was nailed to that cross.

So add to the binding, the falling, and the casting out of Satan also the disarming and defeat of Satan. These are all terms that convey the curtailing of Satan's power that Jesus achieved in His public ministry and death.

The Testimony of Revelation

The decisive passage on the binding of Satan is Revelation 20:1–3, in which it is declared that Satan is "bound" for "a thousand years" (v. 2).

This thousand-year period is popularly known as the Millennium. Revelation 20:1–6 is the only passage in the Bible that makes mention of this era, but it refers to it a total of five times (vv. 2,3,4,5,6).

The prevalent belief among evangelicals for a very long time now has been that the Millennium is in the future. More specifically, it has been widely held that the Millennium is a literal 1,000-year period that begins after the Lord Jesus returns in great glory and binds Satan. This is regarded as a time of perfect peace, when the wolf and the lamb will dwell together (Isa. 11:6; 65:25). It will end, we are told, with the Lord Jesus conducting The Great White Throne Judgment which will result in sinners being cast into the lake of fire (Rev. 20:11–15) and the saints being admitted into their eternal home (Rev. 21:1–22:5).

Many say this of the wolf and lamb verses: "These verses will be fulfilled during the thousand years that Christ will reign on the earth." But the terms "thousand years" or "Millennium" aren't found in those passages. There are, however, clear references to "new heavens and a new earth" (Isa. 65:17; 66:22).

That which many consider to be descriptions of the Millennium are actually descriptions of eternity for believers in Christ. The eternal home of Christians won't be "up there somewhere." It will rather be life on this earth after the Lord has cleansed and purified it. The eternal home of the Christian will be this earth being put back to where it was before sin entered. And every Scripture that is often interpreted as a description of a literal 1,000-year period of peace on earth can well be understood as a description of the Christian's eternal home.

If the Millennium is actually the gospel age, that age extending from Jesus' first coming to His second coming, in what sense can we say that Satan is bound? William Hendriksen writes: " . . . the devil is not bound in *every sense*. . . . Satan's power is curbed and his influence curtailed *with respect to one definite sphere of activity: 'that he should deceive the nations no more.'*"[11] (italics are his).

Hendriksen further says of Satan:

With respect to this one thing he is definitely and securely bound. He cannot destroy the church as a mighty missionary organization heralding the Gospel to all nations.[12]

Since the first coming of Christ, Satan has been bound

11 William Hendriksen, *More Than Conquerors*, Baker Book House (Grand Rapids, MI), 1968, 228.
12 Ibid., 229.

in this one sense: he has been unable to defeat the *witness* of the church since Jesus came.

Keep that word *witness* in mind and think about what has happened since the Lord Jesus ascended to the Father in heaven: Christianity has gone from a tiny group of believers in the little nation of Israel to a worldwide phenomenon with millions and millions of people who profess it. Think about:

- the great number of churches that have been established;
- the large number of Christian institutions (universities, hospitals, seminaries, and benevolence organizations) that have been founded;
- the impressive number of Christian publishing houses and the abundance of Bibles, books, and pamphlets they have produced and are producing;
- the mission organizations that have sent thousands and thousands of missionaries to nations around the world;
- the translation of the Bible and Christian books into many languages;
- the number of Christian radio and television programs;
- the influence of Christian principles on the founding and governance of various nations.

All of these things pertain to the *witness* of the church and may very well cause us to ask if they would have happened if Satan were not bound. Conversely, what would have happened if Satan had been left unbound? Would he not have stopped all of these things?

11

Mr. Super Demon-Possessed

Please Read:
2 Thessalonians 2:1–12

Satan has his demons, and he has used them through the running centuries. In some eras, the devil and his demons have been more active than in others. In the ministry of Jesus and the early church, they were super-active.

Another period of heightened activity will be at the end of the gospel age. Revelation 9:1–11 describes "the bottomless pit" being opened, smoke billowing out, and locusts coming upon the earth. This picturesque language describes an explosion of demonic activity. These "locusts" come from the bottomless pit, and the "king over them" is identified as "Abaddon" and "Apollyon" (v. 11).

These names, one Hebrew and the other Greek, mean "destroyer." They are names for Satan. The demons of hell are pictured as locusts to convey their great number and their capacity for destruction.

This explosion of demonism will occur during the tribulation period, which will follow the gospel age.

The major feature of this tremendous burst of the demonic is one individual in particular—the demon-possessed Antichrist. He will be Mr. Super Demon-Possessed.

The Man of Sin

The apostle Paul called the Antichrist "the man of sin" (2 Thess. 2:3). Paul was asserting that sinfulness would be the dominant feature of his life. It would be his distinguishing trait. It would be as typical or characteristic of him as warmth is of the sun and whiteness is of snow.

And what is sin? It is refusing to conform to the laws of God. We find the very essence of those laws in the Ten Commandments (Ex. 20:1–17). God is our Creator. We are not on this earth by accident. We are not the products of chance. As our Creator, God has the right to tell us that He wants us to live in a certain way. Our Creator is also our Lawgiver.

All of us are lawbreakers. We have all refused to live the way God wants us to live. The only person who never broke any of God's laws was the Lord Jesus Christ. He was perfect in thought, in word, and in deed.

Jesus, the perfect law keeper, is also the One who can provide forgiveness for our lawbreaking.

The Antichrist will be to law-breaking what the Lord Jesus was to law-keeping.

Since sin entered the human race, the spirit of Antichrist has been present and at work. Paul declared that "the mystery of lawlessness is already at work" (2 Thess. 2:7). The apostle John referred to "the spirit of the Antichrist, which you have heard was coming and is now already in the world" (1 John 4:3).

But that spirit of Antichrist, which has been present all along in this sinful world, will find its full and complete expression in the Antichrist at the end of the gospel age. He will be the great lawbreaker. He will hate the laws of God with utmost hatred and will take delight in sneering at them and flagrantly casting them aside. He will enshrine the breaking of God's laws as the centerpiece of his reign, approving of and promoting those who agree with him, and fiercely persecuting those who don't. People have always taken "pleasure in unrighteousness" (2 Thess. 2:12), but never to the degree that they will during the reign of the Antichrist.

Paul stated that the Antichrist will be revealed when something is "taken out of the way" (2 Thess. 2:7). That something may very well be civil law. Paul may have been saying that there will be a breakdown of law and order in the world before the Antichrist is revealed. The way in which he will come to power may be through restoring law. If so, it will not be God's law, which he will hate, but his own law.

The Deceiver and Persecutor

The Antichrist will be stunningly successful. Most of the world's citizens will embrace him with a wild and fanatical devotion. He will evidently declare himself to be God and will be enabled by Satan to work signs and wonders (2 Thess. 2:9). He will also be a master of deception. With his wonder-working powers and his deception, the Antichrist will be quite a package. And the vast majority—practically all—will fall for him hook, line, and sinker.

The prophet Daniel was given a preview of an Antichrist who would arise in the form of one Antiochus Epiphanes. This man persecuted the Jews from 171 to 165 BC. The description of this particular Antichrist certainly makes us look beyond him to the final Antichrist. We are told that Antiochus' power would be "mighty," but it would not be his own. In other words, his power would come from Satan. We are also told that he would "destroy fearfully."

Specifically, he would destroy "the holy people." He would "understand sinister schemes" and would be "cunning." Furthermore, he would "magnify himself in his heart." The best part of the description is that Antiochus would be "broken without human hand," that is, he would be broken by God (Dan. 8:23–26). All of these details apply even more to the great Antichrist at the end of time.

Where will God be in all of this? If we think He will be entirely absent from the scene, we are wrong. Quite the opposite! When the Antichrist steps on the human stage, God Himself will "send them a strong delusion, that they should believe the lie" (2 Thess. 2:11). Satan has always trafficked in lies. He is the great liar, but his master lie will be that the Antichrist is God. And people will believe it.

Are you wondering why God will further the rule of the Antichrist by giving people the "strong delusion" of which Paul spoke? It will be God's judgment! After a prolonged period in which people have stubbornly refused to believe God's truth, He will judge them by making them incapable of believing it. He will take them from not being willing to not being able!

But there is more to it than that. Yes, accepting the lie of the Antichrist will be God's judgment, but it will also be a matter of God bringing things down to the end so that the true Christ will be glorified.

Is the Antichrist near? He may very well be. There are converging lines. The love of people for those with celebrity status, the increasing desire for globalization, the growing contempt for Christianity, the craving for sensational things, the ongoing breakdown of morality, the continuing development of technology that enables information to be disseminated worldwide in seconds, the interconnectedness of millions of people through social media, the ever-increasing emphasis on political correctness—all these things will have to be in place in order for the Antichrist to come to power. The stage for the Antichrist's performance seems to be very close to being completely set.

12

The
Final Victory

Please Read:
Revelation 19:11–21

F rederick S. Leahy calls it "the protracted struggle."[13] It began on this earth centuries ago. The antagonists have been God, His Son, the Holy Spirit, the good angels, and God's people on one hand, and Satan and his demons on the other. It started when God promised to send His Son as the Seed of the woman (Gen. 3:15). Satan immediately set himself to "devour her Child" (Rev. 12:4), trying to find a way to keep the Messiah from coming. Failing in that, he tried to destroy the Christ child, and, failing in that, he tried to get Jesus to derail His messiahship.

The outcome of the struggle has never been in doubt, but it has been real nonetheless.

The Prelude to the Final Victory

This gospel age, as we have noted, is the era in which Satan is bound. How will this age end? John answers in these words:

> Now when the thousand years have expired, Satan will be released from his prison and will go out to deceive the nations which are in the four corners of the earth. . .
> (Rev. 20:7–8a)

---

13 Leahy, *The Victory of the Lamb*, 27.

So Satan, who is bound now in terms of the spreading of the gospel, will be bound no longer. He who "should deceive the nations no more till the thousand years were finished" (Rev. 20:3) will "go out to deceive the nations" (Rev. 20:7). The good news is that he will be able to do this deceiving for only "a little while" (Rev. 20:3). So we can call this period "Satan's little season." Satan, who is bound during the gospel age, will not always be bound.

This season will be short, but it will also be horrendous. It will be marked by three dreadful events:

- the great apostasy;
- the great tribulation;
- the reign of the Antichrist.

The question that comes surging forward to demand an answer begins with that pesky word "Why?". Why will God bring the gospel age to an end by releasing Satan for a little season? It's always tricky and probably more than a little foolish to attempt to answer questions that have both "why" and "God" in them. God has His purposes and His plans, and He is under no obligation to explain them to us. The good news is that God will make all things clear to His people in eternity, and it will all make such perfect sense that all His people will say of Him: "He has done all things well."

In this life, we want to read the book of God's providence (how God governs the world). But God tells us to read the book of His promises now (the Bible), and in heaven He will finally read to us the book of His providence.

We have a tendency to say to God: "Please explain Yourself now, and we will trust and obey." But God says: "Please trust and obey, and I will explain Myself later."

On the "why" of Satan's release, we have to agree with Gary Benfold:

> We do not know why God will allow this release; we are not told. We know that God is always in control, even of Satan, and we know that sometimes—for good and wise purposes—God allows evil to prosper.[14]

It is clear from John's words that Satan will enjoy tremendous success during his little season. The phrase "the four corners of the earth" indicates that the whole world will be caught up in the deception.

That brings us to what we can call "the fog around Gog and Magog" (Rev. 20:7-8). We can call it "fog" because there has been so much controversy and confusion about Gog and Magog. Some try to connect these names with specific nations. To get some clarity on this matter, let's turn to Benfold again:

> Specifically, who are Gog and Magog? It is a reference to Ezekiel 38 and 39, where Ezekiel prophesies the terrible persecution that was to come under Antiochus Epiphanes, the ruler of Syria. In about 170 BC there was an astonishing onslaught against godliness in Israel and ferocious persecution broke out. It was very brief: it was only a little season. Yet while it lasted it was ferocious indeed. Gog in Ezekiel is the evil prince of Magog—or Syria—and because the persecution was both fierce and brief, the names are used here to symbol-

14 Gary Benfold, *Revelation Revealed*, Day One Publications (Leominster, UK), 2005, 168.

ize the last great outbreak of evil. . . . It is a time when the armies of the world will gather against God. Opposition will be worldwide and things will look bleak indeed for the church of Jesus, but it is the last attack of the forces of evil against the church. . . . Then suddenly, when it looks as if the church cannot possibly survive, it all comes to an end.[15]

The Nature of the Final Victory

Satan's "little season" will be brought to a dramatic halt by the Lord Jesus Christ at "the place called in Hebrew, Armageddon" (Rev. 16:16). By the way, this is the only verse in the Bible in which the word "Armageddon" is found.

What is the meaning of this word in Hebrew? Leon Morris makes the point that it may refer to the mount of Megiddo (*har*—mount, *megiddo*—Megiddo) or to the city of Megiddo (*ir*—city, *megiddo*—Megiddo).[16]

This much is clear: the word is associated with Megiddo, which has been the site of some pivotal battles.

The first of these battles may very well have been when Israel, led by Deborah, went against the Canaanite army, which boasted of its nine hundred chariots of iron. If we had been there to witness the unfolding of this battle, we would have said: "Israel has no hope!" But God intervened on behalf of Israel, and the Canaanites were decisively defeated (Judg. 4:1–24). Yes, this battle was fought at Megiddo (Judg. 5:19).

So *Armageddon* has come down to us as a word that depicts God suddenly stepping in to deliver His people when they find themselves facing certain defeat at the

15 Ibid., 169.
16 Leon Morris, *Tyndale New Testament Commentaries: The Revelation of St. John*, William B. Eerdmans, Grand Rapids, MI., p199

hands of a far superior enemy.

The Bible gives us other instances of this very thing (1 Samuel 17; 2 Kings 3; 6:1–18; 6:24–7:8; Isaiah 36:1–37:38).

So we can say that there have been Armageddons in history, but those cannot begin to compare to the one that will occur at the end of time. That will be the last of all the Armageddons and the greatest of them all.

Revelation 16:12–14 sets the stage for us. The "great river Euphrates" will be dried up "so that the way of the kings from the east might be prepared" (v. 12). And "three unclean spirits like frogs" will come out of the mouths of the dragon, the beast, and the false prophet (v. 12).

What is all this? The Euphrates River represents Babylon, and Babylon represents the world's opposition to God and His people. The river being dried up suggests that everything that has kept the world from destroying every last believer in Christ will finally be removed. Then we have the three spirits like frogs coming out of the mouths of the dragon (Satan), the beast (anti-Christian government) and the false prophet (anti-Christian religion). What are to make of this? The mouths represent speaking, and the speaking, we assume, reflects what is in the minds. And what do the dragon, the beast, and the false prophet have on their minds except plots, schemes, and strategies to use against the church?

The three spirits and the frogs tell us what these plots, schemes, and strategies are like. The three spirits represent demons or that which is hellish in nature. The plans initiated by the devil and set in motion through anti-Christian government and anti-Christian religion will be hellish in nature. They will be hatched in hell and sent out of the gates of hell against the church.

The frogs represent that which is vile, filthy, and disgusting, and so are the schemes that Satan uses against God's people.

What a picture! The dragon uses the beast and the false prophet to implement hellish, foul plans against the church, and he is effective in doing so that all obstacles to attacking Christianity are finally removed. The way is clear! And success seems to be certain! Satan's plans are so clever! His power is so great! And the church is so weak! Now, at last, the world will forever rid itself of every last vestige of the Christian faith!

But then Armageddon! The Lord Jesus Christ will graciously, powerfully, and gloriously intervene on behalf of His beleaguered church and will turn what appeared to be sure defeat into stunning victory. The tables will be turned. The soon-to-be vanquished will be the eternal victors. And the Christ so hated by the world will be seen to be

KING OF KINGS
AND LORD OF LORDS.
(Rev. 19:16)

If anyone is inclined to visualize Armageddon as a battle with first one side prevailing and then the other and with the outcome in doubt, he or she should ponder Paul's promise regarding the Lord's victory over the Antichrist:

. . . whom the Lord will consume with the breath of His mouth and destroy with the brightness of His coming.
(2 Thess. 2:8)

When the Lord intervenes to deliver His people in the final Armageddon, it will be swift, stunning (to the wicked), and devastating. In other words, Satan's short season will end with the Lord making short work of him. Jesus' victory over him will be quick, total, and glorious. Let us make sure now that we will be on the winning side then. And the only way to be on the winning side is by repenting of our sins and trusting completely in the Lord Jesus Christ.

Part IV—Christians and Demons

13

Spiritual Warfare

Please Read:
Ephesians 6:10–20

Christians eagerly await the final triumph of the Lord Jesus Christ over the devil and all of his demons, but waiting doesn't mean that they are sitting in idleness. While they wait, they wage war. Charles R. Erdman says:

> The Christian life is a continual conflict. Battle must be waged daily against the most relentless foes. In this warfare there is no discharge.[17]

The most detailed description we have of the Christian's warfare is found in Paul's letter to the Ephesians. Paul's presentation of this falls into three easily discernible categories: the foe to be faced, the armor to be appropriated, and the praying to be practiced.

The Foe to Be Faced (v. 12)

Our enemy, as we have been noting all along, is Satan along with his evil empire. Paul isn't denying that when he uses the terms "principalities," "powers," "the rulers of the darkness of this age," and "spiritual hosts of wickedness." He is rather giving us additional insight into the awful nature of our foes and their ways of operating. They must not be taken lightly. Those who joke about the

17 Charles R. Erdman, *The Epistle of Paul to the Ephesians* (The Westminster Press, Philadelphia, PA), 121.

devil and his forces simply don't understand what they're talking about.

"Principalities" refers to ruling dignitaries or principal rulers. The demons constitute an army, which is well ordered with some demons having authority over other demons.

"Powers" tells us that the various titles and roles that demons may have aren't meaningless. The principalities actually possess great power and authority.

"The rulers of the darkness of this age" means that all the wrongs, all the ignorance, all the misery of this world are not mere happenstance. They have come about because demonic forces have ordered, encouraged, and promoted these things.

"Spiritual hosts of wickedness in the heavenly places" shows us that the forces we are up against are in the spiritual realm. In "heavenly places" means they aren't on our earthly level. Although they operate on this earth, they are not earthly in nature.

It's only as we recognize the true nature of our enemy that we can effectively fight. The fact that Paul says, "We do not wrestle against flesh and blood" must not be taken to mean that Christians are never opposed by mere men. They often are. It's rather the recognition that the men and women who do oppose us have, behind them, invisible demonic forces who are the true and far greater enemy.

And the fact that Paul uses the word "wrestle" conveys to us the personal, intimate nature of this conflict. The church as a whole is involved in this conflict, but so are individual Christians.

The Armor to Be Appropriated (vv. 13–17)

The apostle's description of our foes is so dreadful and fearful that we might be tempted to think we have absolutely no hope of succeeding against them. That's not the case. Paul doesn't admonish his readers to flee; he rather gives his readers a threefold call to "stand" (vv. 11,13,14).

How can we stand against such a frightening foe? We have armor, and Paul lays before us its various parts. The first three items are to be put on and the last three are to be taken up.

Parts to Be Put On

What are the items that are to be worn on the body? They are the belt of truth, the breastplate of righteousness, and the shoes of peace (vv. 14–15).

What is *the belt of truth?* Peter Jeffrey gives this answer: "The belt signifies unqualified confidence in the truth of Scripture. This is the foundation of everything."[18]

To put it another way, the person who doesn't hold to the truth of God's Word is exactly the person that demonic forces are looking to assail. The person who is always "up in the air" about the teachings of the Bible will soon be "down in the dirt" under the heel of the devil.

Putting on *the breastplate of righteousness* means we are to constantly remind ourselves that believers are clothed in the perfect righteousness of the Lord Jesus Christ. His righteousness has been put to our account. This is vital because one part of the devil's assault on us is to constantly remind us that we are so unrighteous in and of ourselves that we don't belong in the Lord's army. A Christian who is unsure of his or her salvation makes a very poor soldier,

18 Peter Jeffrey, *Opening up Ephesians* (Evangelical Press, Darlington, UK), 2002, 72.

but those who point the devil to the perfect righteousness of Christ soon find that he isn't anxious to continue the battle.

The shoes of peace tell us that we can't withstand the devil's force if we are slipping and sliding. To stand our ground, we must have solid footing. To have solid footing means we must be sure that we have peace with God, and we have that in and through the gospel of Christ. We can't be at war with the devil if we are wondering whether we are at peace with God. The precious gospel is our sufficient answer to all of the devil's accusations.

Parts to Be Taken Up (vv. 16–17)

The first piece of the armor to be taken up is *the shield of faith*. This shield is to be used to "quench all the fiery darts of the wicked one" (v. 16). The fiery darts are the doubts, unholy thoughts, skeptical thoughts, vain imaginations, and anxieties that the devil embeds in our minds. The only way they can be quenched and dislodged is by holding up the shield of faith. Faith is believing what God has said in His Word. When the devil urges us to believe his insinuations, the Christian must answer: "I believe what the Lord has said." In God's Word, there is comfort for every anxiety and there is confidence for every doubt.

The second piece of the armor that we are to take up is *the helmet of salvation*. In 1 Thessalonians 5:8, Paul identifies the Christian's helmet as "the hope of salvation." The Christian soldier can't fight successfully against Satan if he or she doesn't have the hope of victory. There's always an element of uncertainty in the current use of the word "hope." Someone tells us that he or she is hoping to get a good report from the doctor, and we immediately conclude that this person is expressing uncertainty. In the New Testament, the word "hope" doesn't include any uncertainty. It is always certain hope! It means that we are not only absolutely sure of our outcome but also eagerly looking forward to it.

The sword of the Spirit is the Word of God. Yes, we have already encountered that in the belt of truth, but it's different here. God's Word as the belt of truth enables us to withstand Satan's attacks. As the sword of the Spirit, it enables us to put him to flight even as the Lord Jesus did when He was tempted by the devil. All of the Christian's armor is defensive in nature except the sword of the Spirit. It is the only offensive weapon we need.

The Praying to Be Practiced (vv. 18–20)

Paul closes his powerful and insightful presentation of spiritual warfare by calling on his readers to pray. Prayer isn't another piece of the armor. It is rather something to be done in conjunction with the use of the whole armor.

The word "all" is our key for understanding the praying that we are to do. We are to pray at all times, in all ways (using all forms or kinds of prayer), with all perseverance (not playing out or giving up) and for all the saints.

John R.W. Stott observed: "Most Christians pray sometimes, with some prayers and some degree of perseverance, for some of God's people."[19]

Surely, we can do better than this!

---

19 John R.W. Stott, *The Bible Speaks Today: The Message of Ephesians* (Leicester, UK), 1979, 283.

14

A Practical Question[20]

Please Read:
2 Timothy 3:14–17

20 Much of this chapter may also be found in my book *Our Great God of Wonders*, Day One Publications (Leominster, UK), 2015, 10–14.

The devil and demons hate the Bible and endeavor to keep people from reading it, believing it, and obeying it. The Bible clearly teaches us about demons. Can we really be sure that the Bible is God's Word?

As I pointed out at the end of chapter five, some will observe that all the evidences I mentioned to prove the reality of demons come from the Bible. They wonder why we should believe the Bible. How can we know that a book so old is really reliable? They may also observe that very few believe the Bible in these days. "So," they say, "if you believe the Bible, you have to believe in demons, but if you don't believe the Bible, all the evidence for demons vanishes."

Many who doubt the truth of Scripture think that those who believe it do so merely because they *want* it to be true. In other words, they think those who trust the Bible have no legitimate reasons for doing so. Is that indeed the case? Or are there solid and substantial reasons for believing the Bible is actually God's Word? Our emphatic answer is that there are several compelling reasons for accepting the authority of the Bible.

The Bible's Correspondence to What We See around Us

As we look at the world in general and our nation in particular, we see hatred, disunity, crime, wars, political corruption, immorality, instability, and addictions of various kinds.

The Bible alone gives us the explanation for all of these things. It tells us that men and women were created by God, but they are no longer as God made them. Although we were made as God's special creatures, we have refused to live in obedience to Him. We are sinners. What is sin? It is refusing to conform to the laws of God.

One of the great ironies of our day is that so many deny the reality of sin while they engage in behavior each day that acknowledges it. When we lock our doors, we admit the reality of sin. When we sign a contract, we do the same. When we install cameras to monitor our houses and grounds, we declare the truth of human sinfulness. Why do we use passwords on our electronic devices and shred important documents if we don't believe in the reality of sin? Every policeman, attorney, judge, and court of law confronts us with the fact of sin, as does every mortician, funeral home, and cemetery.

The Bible's explanation for our world lines up perfectly with what we observe in this world. That alone should convince us of the truth of the Bible.

The Fulfillment of Biblical Prophecies

The Old Testament has many prophecies regarding various nations and cities, all of which have been fulfilled. In his book *Science Speaks,* Peter W. Stoner cites eleven of these along with the mathematical probabilities of their fulfillment. There is only one word for the probabilities—stunning![21]

The greatest prophecies of the Old Testament are those pertaining to the Messiah. It has been estimated that Jesus fulfilled 325 prophecies. Peter W. Stoner shows that the statistical probability of one man fulfilling only eight of those prophecies is astronomical—1 in 100,000,000,00 0,000,000,000,000,000,000,000![22] Think of this number in light of all 325 Old Testament prophecies!

The Bible's Amazing Unity

The incredible unity of the Bible is one of those reasons. It was produced over a period of 1,600 years by more than forty authors. These men came from many walks of life and represented various levels of learning. David and Solomon were kings. Paul was a scholarly rabbi. Peter and John, on the other hand, were common, ordinary fishermen, and Matthew was a tax collector.

But all of these men contributed to a book that has only one theme—God's salvation of sinners through the redeeming work of His Son.

The Testimony of Jesus

As impressive as these evidences are, no single one qualifies as the main reason Christians believe the Bible. That reason is this: Jesus Himself put His stamp of approval on the entire Bible. This means a couple of things. One is that He endorsed the Old Testament, which was already in place when He was engaged in His earthly ministry. The other is that He pre-endorsed the New Testament before it was written.

21 Peter W. Stoner, *Science Speaks* (Wheaton, IL: Van Kampen Press, 1952), 65.
22 Stoner, 75

Regarding the Old Testament

His endorsement of the Old Testament came in several ways. First, He used it in such a way as to indicate that He regarded it as the final court of appeal. When Satan tempted Him in the wilderness, Jesus defeated him by quoting Scripture (Matt. 4:1–11).

Jesus also confounded the religious leaders of His time by appealing to Scripture. Perhaps the most noteworthy of these occasions came when He answered the Sadducees' question about the bodily resurrection by appealing to the verb tense of an Old Testament passage! (See Matt. 22:23–33).

Secondly, Jesus explicitly affirmed the reliability of the Old Testament. When He wanted to talk about the certainty of Scripture being fulfilled, He selected the smallest character of the Hebrew alphabet (Matt. 5:17–18). On another occasion, He emphatically asserted: "Scripture cannot be broken" (John 10:35).

He was affirming that Scripture cannot be proven to be wrong at so much as a single point.

Thirdly, and perhaps most striking of all, Jesus went out of His way to certify those parts of the Old Testament that are most often dismissed as myths. Adam and Eve (Matt. 19:4–5), Noah and the ark (Matt. 24:37–39), the fiery judgment on Sodom and the terrible fate of Lot's wife (Luke 17:28–32), the miraculous ministries of Elijah and Elisha (Luke 4:25–27), and Jonah and the great fish (Matt. 12:39–41)—all were treated by Jesus as historical facts.

Regarding the New Testament

How could Jesus have endorsed the New Testament before it was written? The answer is that Jesus gave His disciples the assurance that the Holy Spirit Himself would supervise each part of the writing of the New Testament.

The New Testament consists of three parts. The Gospels and the book of Acts are historical in nature. Those writers would need accurate recollection of events.

The Epistles are doctrinal in nature. They were designed to impart instruction and guidance for our believing and behaving. Those writers would need keen insight into the truths of God.

The book of Revelation is concerned to some degree with things to come (Rev. 1:19). Its author would need insight into the future.

The night before He was crucified, Jesus assured His disciples that the Holy Spirit would provide them with each of those needed elements. He would call things to their remembrance (John 14:26). He would guide them into all truth (John 16:13). And He would disclose to them things to come (John 16:13).

So no matter where we turn in Scripture, we may rest assured that the Lord Jesus Himself has, as it were, initialed every page!

But why should we accept the testimony of Jesus regarding the Bible? The answer is that it is obvious that Jesus was no ordinary man. The miracles that He performed and the teachings that He proclaimed made it abundantly evident that He was exactly the person He claimed to be, that is, God in human flesh.

And the crowning proof of that is Jesus' resurrection. Ordinary men do not come out of their graves. But Jesus came out of His! And that indisputably proves, as Paul says, that He is "the Son of God with power" (Rom. 1:4).

How do we know He arose from the dead? The tomb was empty. Many people saw Him. Many lives were changed by the risen Christ. Presented with such evidence, any unbiased jury could hand down only one verdict—Jesus arose!

With such evidence for such a person, does it not make sense to accept His testimony regarding the Bible? Even if it means I must set aside the conclusions of thousands of scholars, I will accept the testimony of Jesus. His credentials put Him in a class by Himself.

The Testimony of the Holy Spirit

While the above proofs are certainly valid, they are not sufficient in and of themselves to convince us that the Bible is the Word of God. In the last analysis, it takes the Spirit of God bearing witness to Scripture to do that, as indicated by the Westminster Confession of Faith:

> . . . we are completely persuaded and assured of the infallible truth and divine authority of the Bible only by the inward working of the Holy Spirit, Who testifies by and with the word in our hearts.[23]

In other words, we do not believe the Bible simply because the Bible tells us to believe the Bible, but rather because the Spirit of God tells us to believe it as we read it. While the external proofs are compelling, it is this internal persuasion that is decisive.

In addition to these evidences, we could also cite the following:

23 *The Westminster Confession of Faith: An Authentic Modern Version* (Signal Mountain, TN: Summertown Texts, 1984), 4.

- its survival even though it has been fiercely attacked;
- the changed lives of those who believe the Bible and seek to obey it;
- the astounding discoveries of archaeologists that corroborate the details of events in the Bible.

With all these impressive evidences in hand, we should most certainly accept what it tells us about the devil and his demons. The Bible is so trustworthy that if only one of its verses affirmed the existence of Satan and his empire, it would be enough. As we have seen, there are many such verses in the Bible. In fact Satan is mentioned in nine books of the Old Testament and by every New Testament author.

15

More Practical Questions

Please Read:

Mark 5:1–20

How Much Control Does Satan Have over This World?
....

W e have seen that Satan is a very powerful and deceitful foe. The Bible warns us about "the wiles of the devil," and it urges us to resist him.

But we must not give the devil more credit than he is due. Some do this. They remember that Paul referred to Satan as "the god of this world" (2 Cor. 4:4, KJV), and they take that to mean that he, the devil, has absolute control over this world. They see God being completely shut out of His own world and being able to accomplish very little.

When the devil was tempting Jesus, he boastfully proclaimed that he had dominion over the world and had the authority to transfer that dominion to Jesus. Frederick S. Leahy calls this Satan's "swaggering pretension," and writes:

> Our Lord knew that Satan was a usurper, arrogating powers to himself which he did not possess. Satan's claim to have dominion over "the kingdoms of the world" is a lie. It is God, not the arch-pretender, who holds the world in His hand.[24]

---

24 Leahy, *Satan Cast Out*, 43.

Leahy then includes what J.N. Geldenhuys has to say about Satan and his supposed total control of the world:

> It is, indeed, true that by God's permission the kingdoms of the world (in so far as sin rules in the hearts and lives of the leader and also of the individual members of the nations) have been delivered to him. Thus Jesus Himself spoke of him as the prince of this world. But He did not mean it in an absolute sense as the arch-deceiver himself pretended. Only to the extent that mankind surrender themselves in sin to the evil one does God permit him to rule over the world of men, but nevertheless always under His highest and final overruling, so that everything in the end leads to His glory. God never lets the reins slip out of His hands.[25]

Yes, Satan has power, but he is never free to exercise that power in an absolute way. He is always subject to God's permission, as we see in the first two chapters of the book of Job. Think for a moment about how much worse this world would be if Satan had complete dominion over this world and could exercise absolute power. There would be no Bibles, no true churches, and no Christians.

So what was Paul saying when he called Satan "the god of this world"? In using the word "god," Paul wasn't attributing any divine attributes to Satan. Satan is a god in this sense alone—he is treated as such by those who don't know Christ. He, Satan, blinds their minds, rules their affections, and secures their obedience. With the phrase

25 Ibid., 44.

"this world," Paul was referring to the world of sinful people. Satan is the god over that world—the wicked world.

We are all born into this wicked world, but Christians have been delivered from it by the grace of God that enlightens the mind, elevates the affections, and energizes the will. The apostle John says: "For whatever is born of God overcomes the world. And this is the victory that has overcome the world—our faith. Who is he who overcomes the world, but he who believes that Jesus is the Son of God?" (1 John 5:4–5).

This brings us to ask again why God allows the devil any power at all. This is, as they say, above our pay grade. We don't understand the ways of God. So let's put our "Why?" questions in our hip pockets and pull them out when we come into the glory of God's presence.

What Are the Marks of Demon Possession?

As we have noted, demons are still active in this world, and there are still cases of demon possession. Missionaries in pagan countries still encounter this phenomenon and bear witness to it. In his book *Satan Cast Out*, Frederick S. Leahy drew from the testimonies of missionaries to compile what he referred to as "common marks of possession." They are:

- speaking in a voice which is not that of the victim;
- unusual physical strength;
- obvious conflict within the person;
- hostility and fear in the presence of Christ when proclaimed in His Word;
- greatly heightened insight and sensitivity;
- speaking in tongues ;

- in cases of involuntary possession, the same physical and mental disturbances as described in the New Testament;
- in cases of voluntary possession, as with sorcerers and spiritist mediums, phenomenal healings are sometimes achieved.

The first five of these characteristics can quite readily be seen in the demon-possessed man that Jesus encountered in Gadara (Mark 5:1–20).

Leahy concluded this section of his book with these words:

> Evangelical missionaries are convinced of the reality of demon-possession today, and find it one of their greatest challenges and problems.[26]

Should Christians Practice Exorcism?

If we acknowledge that demon possession is still occurring, we are confronted with the question of what individual Christians should do if they are confronted with it. Should they attempt to practice exorcism? The fact that the New Testament epistles don't include exorcism in the lists of spiritual gifts (Rom. 12:6–8; 1 Cor. 12:27–31; Eph. 4:7–16; 1 Peter 4:10–11) and don't include any instructions for the practice of it tells us all that we need to know, namely, that exorcism is not to be practiced.

In the Volume 1 of their *Reformed Systematic Theology*, Beeke and Smalley offer this conclusion regarding the practice of exorcism: " . . . it is best to view exorcism as

26 Ibid., 138.

a special ministry of the apostles and evangelists directly appointed by Christ."[27]

We should also note that the Bible nowhere gives us detailed instructions on how to discern demon possession. Some cases of it can be so obvious that no discernment is necessary. Other cases might be less obvious. Believers in Christ must guard against becoming demon-obsessed, and rather focus their attention on prayer and the reading and studying of God's Word.

Can a Christian Be Demon Possessed?

Although we touched briefly on this matter at the close of chapter six, it bears repeating because there are Christians—perhaps many—who are anxious about this.

We don't find the answer to this question by reading what the Bible says about Satan and his demons. We rather find it by reading the Bible's teaching about salvation. If we truly understand God's great work of salvation, we will no longer vex ourselves about whether Christians can be demon possessed.

What is salvation? It is God's glorious work—yes, it is glorious—in which He takes an unbeliever out of Satan's realm and places that person in His, God's, realm. The apostle Paul puts it like this:

He has delivered us from the power of darkness, and translated us into the kingdom of the Son of His love, in whom we have redemption through His blood, the forgiveness of sins.
(Col. 1:13–14)

Paul's word "translated" refers to the practice of

27 Beeke and Smalley, *Reformed Systematic Theology*, 1145.

removing people from one country and settling them as colonists in another. Christians are no longer citizens of Satan's dark and nefarious kingdom. They have been removed from it, and now they are citizens of God's kingdom. Our citizenship is now in heaven (Phil. 3:20).

How does the removing and resettling take place? It is all due to the redeeming work of the Lord Jesus Christ. The very God who refused to grant salvation to the fallen angels devised a way to save mere men and women who are so much lower than the angels. Staggering, isn't it?

God set His love on sinners, and sent "the Son of His love" to provide salvation. This required the Lord Jesus to come to this earth in our humanity. He had to be one of us to do something for us! In that humanity, He lived in perfect obedience to God's holy law. In other words, He lived the life we have refused (and been unable) to live— the life of perfect obedience that God demands. Having lived that perfect life, Jesus went to the cross to die a death such as no one before or since has ever died. It was far more than a mere physical death. While He was on the cross, Jesus actually received the penalty for the sins of all who believe.

God's justice demands that the penalty for sin be paid before He will allow us into heaven. God could not set that penalty aside without violating His own justice. But justice doesn't demand that the penalty be paid twice—only once. So the fact that Jesus paid it on my behalf means I never have to pay it myself. The fact that Jesus bore the eternal wrath that my sins deserve means I will never be the object of God's wrath myself, and I can now triumphantly shout with the apostle Paul: "There is therefore now no condemnation to those who are in Christ Jesus. . ." (Rom. 8:1).

Furthermore, the fact that God would do all this for me in my sins means He will never let me go. He would not pay such a fearful price to save me only to cede His rights of ownership back to Satan. "He who began a good work" in His people "will complete it until the day of Jesus Christ" (Phil. 1:6).

Let's think often of these words from Paul: ". . .I am persuaded that neither death nor life, nor principalities nor powers, nor things present nor things to come, nor height nor depth, nor any other created thing, shall be able to separate us from the love of God which is in Christ Jesus our Lord" (Rom. 8:38–39).

We have encountered those words "principalities" and "powers" before. Paul used them in Ephesians 6:12 as descriptions of the demonic world that we are up against. When we come to Romans 8:38–39 we find those very same words, and the message is loud and clear—our powerful foes are our powerless foes when it comes to reclaiming a child of God.

Because of Jesus' redeeming work, Satan has been decisively and forever defeated in my life. He can never reclaim me or anyone else who belongs to the Lord Jesus. So it seems that the most fitting word with which to close is this: "Hallelujah!"

www.ingramcontent.com/pod-product-compliance
Lightning Source LLC
Chambersburg PA
CBHW071015120626
46546CB00003B/1091